HEALTHY
NEVER TASTED SO GOOD

6/3/17

You are what you eat and Absorb

Susan a Cling
Thank you so much
for your support,
Be well, BeHealthy,
& see ya in either
CO or N.C. :)

CherieMonet

WRITTEN BY
CHÉRIE M. TORRENCE
FOREWORD BY: DR. TANISHA HOOVER

Introduction

Having grown up in North Carolina, I know what good food is and taste like; however I do realize that being healthy and well starts from within. Most body conditions or manifestations such as acne, obesity, diabetes, and cancer, to name a few, that present on the outside of or within the body are a result of what we put in our mouths. Wellness is a state of mind but permeates from what and how we eat. Everything we eat or consume forms and shapes our bodies into what we become. If a person eats starches and carbohydrates, the body soon begins to look fat and soft like the starches they have consumed. If a person eats green vegetable and foods that strengthen and form muscles, they tend to be taller and more lean and muscular than one who has eaten fatty foods that contain starches and carbohydrates. If a person eats foods that are cooked in saturated fats the results soon appear in the texture of the skin in the form of acne or pimples. Our bodies are replicas of what we eat. Consuming healthier, leaner, more nutritional foods results in our bodies reflecting healthier, stronger, leaner frames. It is sad especially when young adults are being diagnosed pre-diabetic or having high enough blood pressures where they have to be put on medications, when if they realize that food our first medicine. "Every bite you take is either fighting disease or feeding it"—Anonymous

This educational cookbook gives recipes that will help insure that a person receives their macro and micro minerals needed. This book also helps one to know what to combine certain spices and foods with to obtain maximum absorption in the body.

All of the meals in this cookbook have been prepared personally and consumed by me. The majority of these meals were made when I was in medical school trying to save money and be creative while preparing different foods and at the same time maintaining my health. While being a student in medical school, "Nutrition" was a course included in my curriculum. I really enjoyed taking this one particular class and learning about all of the essential vitamins and minerals and other healthy nutrients needed daily to maintain a relative degree of health. I am what you call a true "foodie" and I really enjoy good food. I enjoy trying and creating tasty and healthy recipes, and at the same time knowing I'm being good to my body and giving it what it needs.

Preface

One must change their mindset when incorporating changes to their lifestyle, especially in the food they eat every day. Every day we have a choice in what we eat; either to eat what is good and nutritional or to eat "junk" that has no nutritional value. If we are going to try to prolong our lives, it starts with eating healthy and changing our mindsets about what we eat. When we change what we put in our mouths to be healthier, then we change our bodies and how they look and feel. When we change our mindsets, we are also choosing to be healthier without depending on medications to keep us alive.

 It has been said, "You are what you eat, so don't be cheap, fast, or fake." If you/we are truly what we eat, then everything we eat should fuel us and give us energy and not make us tired after consuming a meal. For example, if we put low quality fuel in our vehicles, then we don't get the best mileage out of it.If we use higher quality gasoline, then the vehicle runs smoother and we get a higher performance from it. This is the same for food, drinks, thoughts, and habits that fuel our spirits and bodies. If low quality food is consumed, then the output is low; we are fatigued, we can't think straight or perform at a higher level.

Food is our first, safest, and most powerful medicine. However, food can also be a slow ticket to death. According to health experts and nutritionists, it is always best to buy ORGANIC fruits and vegetables, when possible. Organic is oftentimes more expensive than regular fruits and vegetables, but well worth it. Organic fruits and vegetables don't contain the pesticides, herbicides, or insecticides used to make the fruits and vegetables last longer. Organic foods preserve the body and help keep the body with a youthful glow. After all, you only live once and after a while your body can tell when you are not giving it the best it deserves.

"Let Food be thy medicine, and Medicine be thy Food".—Hippocrates

Did you know that more than 95% of all chronic disease is caused by food choice, toxic food ingredients, nutritional deficiencies and lack of exercise? Mike Adams, the Health Ranger agrees. Of course our grandparents and great grandparents cooked with what they had, but this was before we had GMO's, and everything was over processed. Certain fruits and vegetables that are grown in the ground are grown in pesticide laden soil. This is harmful to our bodies because people are now consuming chemicals with their fruits and vegetables instead of the pure fruit or vegetable. These chemicals play a role in our growth, development, mental capacity, and consequently, contribute to our hormonal disharmonies. These fruits and vegetables have the highest amount of pesticide residue sprayed on them even after delivery to the local food markets/grocery store. This is why apples and other produce are very shiny. Organic foods are healthier for us because they are less exposed to harmful chemicals that infiltrate our bodies and cause cancers or other foreign ailments. To help when shopping, ORGANIC vegetables and fruits are labeled starting with the number 9 on the barcode. There is an app called EWG (Environmental Working Group), and in this app, there is a list of foods called "The Dirty Dozen and The Clean Fifteen", that explains which foods should be purchased Organic and which ones can be excluded

The suggested grocery stores/ food markets are not located in all regions. Suggested grocery stores to purchase food items include:

Trader Joe's
Sprouts
Whole Foods
Farmer's Markets (if one is in your area)

Foreword

We are always trying to find ways to improve our health. That's why the diet/nutrition industry is a multi- billion-dollar industry. We fail to realize that it is not about the next new diet trend but, changing what we eat on a daily basis. With this comes educating yourself, to help change your mindset about food. ***Healthy Never Tasted So Good*** helps to educate you and gives you lots of tasty, quick, healthy recipe options. I recommend this book to anyone who is a "foodie", people wanting to learn healthy recipes, and folks that love to try new foods!

Dr. Tanisha Hoover, NMD, BSN, RN

Acknowledgements

To my **Momma**, who is and continues to be my #1 fan in my life. She is my greatest inspiration. I thank her for being my biggest cheerleader. In fact, my first ideas about nutrition and healthy eating started with her. She also inspired me to research and present my high school Senior Project on "You Are What You Eat."

To **Uncle George,** I thank you for taking a genuine interest in what I am doing and always encouraging me.

To **Aunt Pat,** who has been an encourager and shoulder since I was a baby. You were there for me, even with the ducks! ☺ Thank you for starting me on the path to health. Thank you for your readings of me and seeing what I could not see. Thank you for the continued lessons, the visions, and being an avid supporter in my life.

To **Dr. Amani Flood,** Thank you for seeing and tasting my Rainbow Salad and agreeing that it looked and tasted delicious. Thanks also for giving me the idea to create a book. You are truly the impetus for this publication.

To **Dr. Amanda Roberson,** Thank you for teaching in a way that was like none other. Thank you for having cute pneumonics and ways for students to remember the information.

To My loyal friends, **Dwayne Deloatch,** Thank you for always being a great friend, being consistent, and being supportive and pushing me to follow my dreams wherever they may take me. "I had no idea how much consistency really meant to me, until it mattered."

Danielle Richmond, Thank you for being there for me and traveling to the hottest state that I could have lived in to support me and celebrate milestones in my life.

Dr. Tanisha Hoover, Thank you for being a great friend and "sister from another mother" ☺, for sticking by me and supporting my entire journey through school(s). Thank you also for inspiring me to start cooking more and experimenting in the kitchen.

Ken Grimes, Thank you for your willingness to always learn about something healthy. Your quest and query for knowledge impresses me. "Serous Business" ☺

Dr. Tursha Hamilton, Thank you so much for being the voice of reason as it pertains to how to be an author, and what I should NOT do. Especially with my imagination and pictures for the book ☺

Ms. Sherry Brantley, Thank you for pushing me to finish this book and to continue writing. You are such an inspiring author/mentor. Your unmeasured support has sustained me.

To **Nemmsaiu Amen-Sebek** and my other mentors who have supported me on this journey of life, I THANK YOU!! Please know that I really appreciate you and do not take anything for granted.

Disclaimer: This book was written from the education and knowledge of the author. This book is intended to help one choose better options for their health. This book is merely a book for educational and food preparation purposes only. This book is not intended to be used to diagnose or prescribe medical conditions nor as a replacement for your Physician's medical advice. Please consult your physician if you are unsure about some of these food selections.

Contents

DEDICATION

This book is dedicated to everyone who has a desire to be healthier and have a more vibrant, energetic life. Remember being healthy, is a choice and a mindset.

I hope that this book will enhance your health journey to be and think healthier.

"The groundwork of all happiness is good health"—Leigh Hunt

Breakfast

Veggie Omelet with Turkey Bacon & Spinach

Ingredients:

> 2-3 Free Range Eggs or Organic Eggs
> ¾ cup Soy Milk, Coconut Milk, Almond Milk or Water
> 1 Tbsp Coconut Oil
> 1 handful of Organic Spinach
> 2-3 strips of Nitrate Free Turkey Bacon
> Salt, Pepper, Garlic,
> Cheese

The majority of these recipes serve 1-2 people. Feel free to adjust to your household.

Optional: Red or Yellow peppers, mushrooms

Directions:

Cook 2 strips of Turkey Bacon over medium heat until desired texture is reached. Place turkey bacon aside and let cool. Put coconut oil in the frying pan over medium heat. While the coconut oil is melting beat the egg and put in desired seasonings and milk or water in a bowl and whisk until all ingredients are mixed well. When the pan is ready, pour egg mixture in and let sit for approximately 2 minutes to let the egg form. Once all of the egg liquid is cooked add in spinach, and break the strips of bacon into smaller pieces and add in. Fold egg over to form an omelet.

Side Item:

Feel free to add Watermelon or any fruit to go along with this delicious breakfast.

Why the chosen ingredients?

- Coconut oil is a saturated fatty acid (the good fat that we need) and has what is called Lauric Acid, and is good for just about everything in the body. Lauric Acid has been shown to increase HDL levels of cholesterol. Coconut oil has been shown to reduce the amount of abdominal weight especially in women on a consistent basis. There is evidence that Coconut oil increases nutrient absorption. Coconut oil reduces viruses, and bacteria.

- Free Range eggs means that the hen was not stressed during the birthing of the chicken. A less stressed hen that produces free range eggs means that the hen was able to roam freely vs being caged in under high noise and stress. Free range chickens are also not under antibiotics to make them grow quicker and be ready for faster production. Eggs are a source of essential fatty acids that we need and are a source of Omega-3, and Omega-6 for our body (Alpha lipoic acid and Linoleic acid), especially when hens are fed a free range omega-3 rich diet they may have some increase in DHA and EPA. When DHA and EPA are consumed together this has shown great benefit in reducing Alzheimer's/dementia. Omega-3's in the body help to reduce inflammation and benefit for cholesterol. DHA helps with vision and nervous function.

- Spinach is a great "Super Food" and leafy green vegetable that contain vitamins such as A&K. Super food means that it is high in nutrients and boosts the immune system. Spinach is a metabolism boosting food. Also, spinach is a source of calcium, which is the most abundant mineral in the body.

- It is important to consume nitrate free meats because the nitrate is known to cause stomach cancers and brain damage.

- Watermelon is a good sweet summer fruit that is high in Vitamin A&C. Most fruits with a pink/red color can be used as adjunctive therapy to treat and prevent cancers. Many studies support beta carotene's cancer protective effects particularly in tomatoes, watermelon, and guava.

Hash brown Breakfast Pizza

Ingredients:

    1 Tbs. coconut oil

    Nitrate Free Turkey Sausage

    2-3 eggs

    1 tsp salt

    1 tsp pepper

    1 tsp garlic powder

    2 cups Shredded Hash browns

Optional:

    Milk alternative

    Cheese

    water

Directions:

In a medium sauce pan, put in coconut oil over medium heat. Add hashbrowns and brown on one side. Flip hashbrowns over once browned. In another sauce pan cook Turkey Sausage. While both are cooking whisk together eggs, seasonings, and milk. Cut the turkey sausage into smaller pieces and put into pan with hashbrowns. Pour egg mixture over the hashbrown and sausage. Place pan in the oven on 350º, and bake until golden brown. Pretty good combination of flavors early in the morning.

Turkey Omelet Sandwich

Ingredients:

> 2 Free Range Eggs
> 1 tsp Earth Balance Butter
> 2-3 slices Deli Meat Turkey
> Handful Broccoli
> 1 slice Swiss Cheese
> Onion powder, Garlic, Tumeric, Salt, Pepper
> ½ tsp Milk/water
> Whole wheat bread
> Mayonnaise or *Vegenaise
>
> Salsa
>
> *Vegenaise can be a substitute for traditional Mayonnaise or Miracle whip if there is an egg allergy, and/or for healthier choices. Vegenaise tastes just like regular mayonnaise. There are other varieties of vegenaise such as chipotle, soy free, grape seed oil, to name a few.

Directions:

In a bowl, beat eggs, seasonings, milk/water while pan is heating on medium heat. Once pan is ready add butter. Pour in mixture and let sit until liquid is cooked. Chop up broccoli and add in. Break cheese into pieces and add in. Break turkey into pieces and add in. Flip egg over to form an omelet. On one side of bread add Vegenaise/mayonnaise. Add omelet to bread and you have an omelet sandwich!! A great start to the day (maybe after exercise).

*The active ingredient in Curcumin that is found in turmeric is what aids in fighting long term diseases such as Alzheimer's. When adding turmeric to recipes, the body absorbs it better when added with black pepper.

*Onion and Garlic gives good flavor and seasoning to most meals.

*Earth Balance Butter is a dairy free alternative to traditional butters.

*Broccoli stores all kinds of good vitamins such as Vitamin A, (which alleviates rough skin). Broccoli contains certain B vitamins and Vitamin C (more than citrus). Broccoli also contains these minerals Potassium, Calcium, and Iron. Broccoli reduces inflammation and also helps clear out environmental toxins that we consume daily. If broccoli is lightly cooked, it will keep the chlorophyll which makes it green; counteract the gas that most people experience with this family of vegetables.

Mango Chia Pudding

½ cup Milk alternative (Almond, Hemp, Coconut, etc)
½ cup Organic Chia Seeds
1 Fresh Mango or Organic Frozen Mango

Optional: Granola, Pineapple, Cinnamon, Fresh mint.

In a spill proof container, put milk and add chia seeds, Cut up Mango, or use frozen pieces and put in blender with very little water so that Mangoes become pureed. Add puree mixture to milk and chia seeds and stir. Place mixture in refrigerator for at least 30 minutes so that contents can become gelatinous. Once pudding is formed, it can be topped with Granola.

Factoid:

- Chia seeds are great hormone equalizers, helps normalize blood sugar levels, promotes sound sleep, is a source of calcium, contain Vitamin C, iron, potassium and Omega-3. All valuable nutrients that the body needs and oftentimes is deficient. Chia seeds help with the flow in the body and can aid with constipation because they are high in fiber. Chia mixed with any liquid forms a gelatinous "pudding".

- Pineapples contain Bromelain which aids in the digestive process; help reduce inflammation for joints and contain certain B vitamins. Be careful because Pineapples can be a blood thinner.

Take a sip of Water...

Drinking water should be part of the daily routine. Check with your PCP on how much water is adequate for your body. I know, I get it, water gets boring and is flavorless. Tasty treats can always be added to the water for taste, and other properties. Some suggestions to add to water are lemon (alkalizes the body) cucumber (cooling, helps with weight loss), strawberry, frozen grapes, orange, fresh mint. Drinking room temperature water with lemon first thing at the start of the day jump starts the metabolism and tells the body to wake up. This is a gentle/non shocking approach to waking the body organs up.

Smoothies

On the Go Green Smoothie

Ingredients

    2 cups Milk alternative (Flax, Almond, Coconut, Soy etc) or Water

    1 scoop protein powder* or plain Greek yogurt

    Frozen Fruit or fresh fruits

    2 handfuls Organic Spinach

    1 tsp Cinnamon

    1 Tbsp Spirulina **

Directions:

In a blender, pour in milk or water. Then add scoop of protein powder. If using fresh fruit, chop up and add to blender. If not, add in frozen fruit. Add in spinach. Top with cinnamon. Blend until all ingredients are blended smoothly.

*Protein powder sustains you throughout the day. What's the point of having a smoothie if it doesn't hold you for a couple of hours?!

**Spirulina is an algae good for many different health benefits. Spirulina is high in calcium. It is alkaline forming, cleansing and rejuvenates the liver. Spirulina also helps to reduce stress because it is rich in tryptophan.

Glowing Grape Smoothie

Ingredients:

½ cup water
1 Frozen or Fresh Banana
Handful Frozen Grapes (Red)
2 TBs Plain Greek Yogurt
1 TBs Flax Seed
1 tsp Almonds

1 tsp Cinnamon

Directions:

Pour water in a blender. Add in banana, and grapes. Add in Yogurt, Flax seed, and almonds. Blend until smooth or desired consistency.

Factoid: When consuming flax seeds, make sure to buy the whole seed. The greatest benefit comes when it is freshly ground. This can be done in a blender or coffee grinder when the seed will produce the beneficial nutrients. Flax seeds should be ground up because once ground it has a polyphenol that is found in plants called lignans, which help decrease extra estrogen that is in our bodies. Good for PCOS, Endometriosis, Fibroids, Constipation, etc. Flax is a soluble fiber that also is gelatinous (just like chia seeds) and contain high amounts of fiber.

Cinnamon reduces blood sugar levels.

Almonds are a source of protein, and are the only nut that helps to alkaline the body.

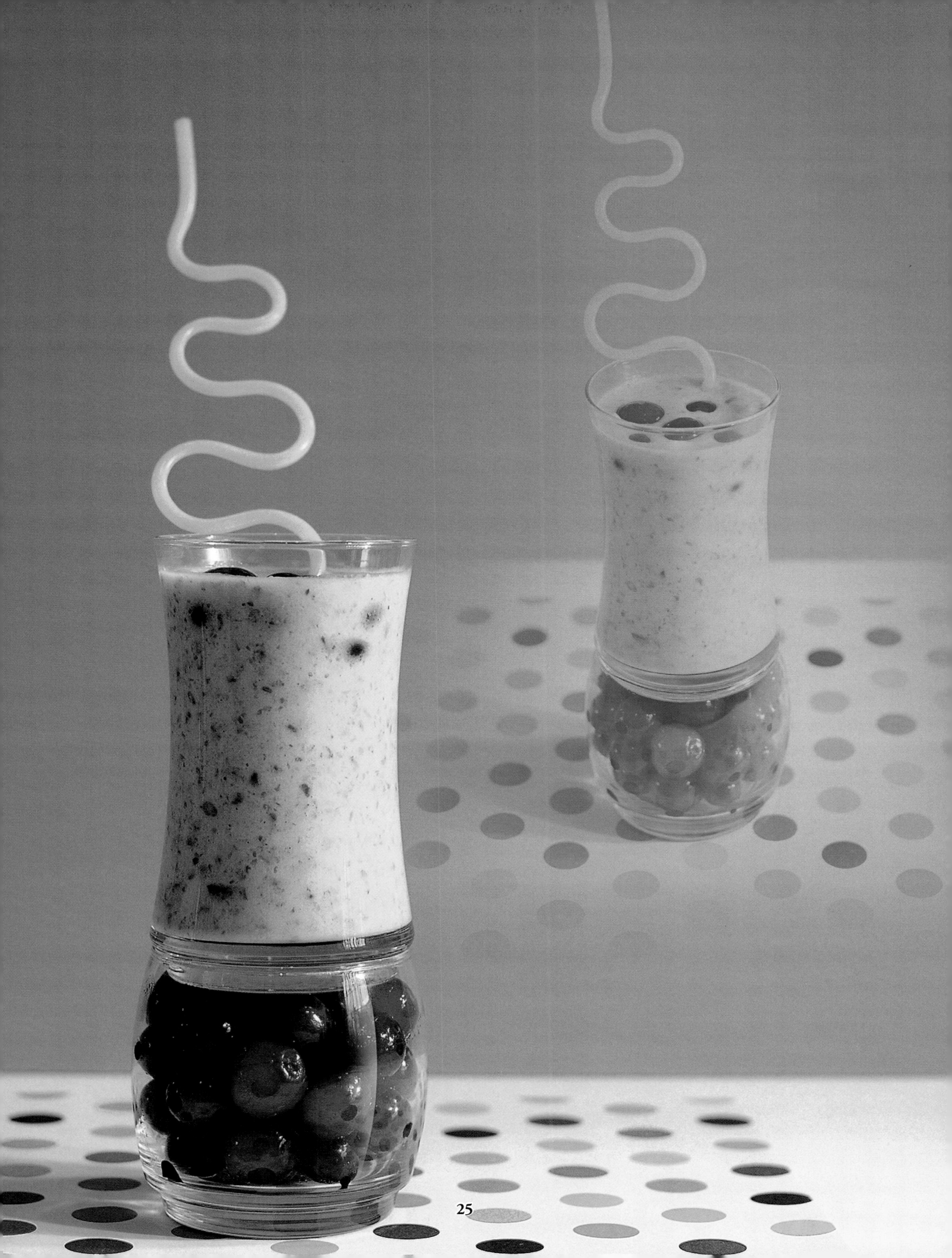

Apple Pie Smoothie

Ingredients:

1 Organic Red/Green Apple

Handful of Slivered Almonds

½ cup of Dried Uncooked Oats or Nut Butter (Almond, Cashew, etc)

Handful of Organic Spinach

Water or Almond Milk

1 tsp of Vanilla Extract

1 tsp Cinnamon

Directions:

- Chop up the apple(s) and spinach. Add to the blender the wet ingredients including the vanilla extract, and then the dry. Then add in the apple, spinach, almonds, cinnamon, and the uncooked oats. A healthy morning apple pie for breakfast!!

- Factoids: As the saying goes "An apple a day keeps the doctor away", so apples are very good for us. Apples are a source of fiber.

- Why Nut Butter instead of Peanut Butter? Peanut Butter has what is called aflotoxins. Aflotoxins are a type of mold that the body does not digest well.

Tropical Colada Smoothie

Ingredients:

½ Banana

½ cup Frozen/Fresh Pineapple

½ cup of Coconut Milk *can be unsweetened or sweetened

¼ cup of Dried Uncooked Oats

1 inch Fresh Ginger

Directions:

Add milk to blender, and then combine all ingredients in a blender until desired texture/consistency. Make sure to cut the ginger into small pieces.

Note: Bananas are a source of potassium, and aids with muscle spasms. Bananas are also a source of Calcium and Magnesium, which aid in heart health.

Blue Brain Booster

Ingredients:

½ Pkg. Wild Frozen or Fresh Blueberries
Handful of Strawberries
Handful of Walnuts
1 cup Flax Seeds
½ cup Milk alternative or water
1 Tbsp Nut Butter (Almond, Sunflower Seed, etc)
½ tsp of Cinnamon
Optional: Goji Berries, Bananas

Directions:

Add in milk alternative/water to blender 1st. Make sure to chop walnuts and strawberries, then add in remainder of ingredients.

- Factoids: Blueberries and any berry are high in antioxidants, and Vitamin C. Because Blueberries are blue, they are known to help with varicose veins.

- Walnuts are shaped like a brain and therefore maximize the brain's function and aids with healthy cell membranes. Walnuts provide essential fatty acids that our bodies need and are high in Omega-3's and is known to help lower cholesterol.

- Goji Berries is another type of Super Food because they are known to help with so many things in the body such as boosting the immune system, and protecting from diseases, and aiding in memory. Goji Berries are known to aid in eye health. They are energy boosters and help maintain a healthy heart because it is rich in Iron. They also help to reduce inflammation/pain.

Juices

Immune Boosting Juice

Ingredients:

> 1 cup water or Orange Juice
> ½ package Pomegranate Seeds
> 1 Orange
> Fresh Pineapple
>
> Fresh Watermelon (with seed is preferred)

Directions

Wash off and peel orange. Add water or orange juice to blender. Cut orange into fourths and add to blender. Cut watermelon out of skin, and cut off skin of pineapple. Add to blender along with other ingredients. Once all ingredients are well blended this juice will appear frothy, but good!

The Ingredients in this recipe contain Vitamin C, and boost the immune system

Salad Dressings

Tasty Salad Dressings

Entice your Taste Buds with these Tasty Salad Dressings

Be aware that when buying salad dressings in the store, they may contain sugars. Try to limit using processed sugars and preservatives in preparing foods, as these lead to disease. It is important to make your own dressing because most over the counter salad dressings contain sugars. According to other health experts, we should consume 0.8 grams of sugar a day. Most times we consume 4-6 times this amount in a day, leading to diseases. Besides, it is fun to experiment with your own creations for salad dressings. It makes a salad more interesting when you can put your own twist to it.

The salad dressings yield about 2-4 oz

Olive Oil & lemon Juice

Directions: Add lemon juice to salad, then top with olive oil and salt. For maximum absorbency, adding an acidic and citrusy juice (lemon, lime, etc) to green vegetables helps to absorb the chlorophyll from the green vegetables

Balsamic Vinegar/Honey

1 tsp of Balsamic Vinaigrette

1 ½ tsp Honey

Directions: Mix ingredients together. Add to salad.

Curry Salad Dressing

1 tsp Curry Paste/Powder

½ juice Lemon

1 tsp Honey

½ tsp ACV (Apple Cider Vinegar)

¼ cup water or olive oil

1Tbs Sunflower Butter or any Nut

Butter alternative

Directions: Add all ingredients to bowl. Mash with a fork until liquid consistency is reached.

Avocado and Basil Dressing

1 Avocado

2-3 sprigs of basil

1 tsp salt

Sprinkle of black pepper

½ cup water or olive oil

Juice of ½ lemon

Directions: Slice avocado in half-length wise. Remove seed, and squeeze avocado into a bowl. Cut sprigs of basil and add to bowl. Add salt, and pepper. Add small amounts of olive oil and water at a time. Mash all ingredients with a fork until the avocado is smooth and creamy. Continue mashing ingredients until desired consistency is reached. Seems to become better the next day. Perfect addition to chicken.

Avocado Lime

1 Avocado

Juice of 1/2 Lime

1 or 2 cloves Garlic

1/4 cup Almond Milk

Salt and pepper to taste

Directions: In a blender, add the almond milk, lime juice, garlic, salt and pepper. Slice avocado in half -length wise, and remove seed. Add to blender.

Blend to desired consistency. Perfect for a taco salad!

This recipe, complimented by Dr. Amani Flood, was the reason this book came to fruition. One day she walked by as I was eating this salad and said, "Ooh, that looks good, what is it?" I replied and said that it was a rainbow salad. She said, "That should be in your cookbook". At that time, I hadn't even thought about a cookbook, I was just trying to stay alive while in medical school.

Rainbow Salad

Ingredients:

Handful of Kale	1 Yellow Pepper
Handful of Spinach	½ bunch Purple Lettuce
1 Red Pepper	Pinch of salt, pepper, garlic powder
1 Red Beet	½ lemon
1 Orange Pepper	½ avocado

Optional:

Broccoli, Chicken,

Dressings: Refer to page 23 for dressing ideas

"When it rains, the crops can grow. The sun comes out and shines down upon us. At the end of every rainbow is not always a pot of gold, but maybe a wealth of health"--Anonymous

Benefits of eating from the rainbow:

Most foods that have color oftentimes correlate to the organs in the body. Red color fruits and vegetables aid in the circulation of the heart. They contain Vitamin C, Lycopene, and Quercetin.

Orange/Yellow foods have vitamins A, C, Beta Carotene, and Potassium. Orange/yellow benefit the skin, eyes, and aids in anti-inflammation.

Green Foods contain Vitamin K, Folate, Iron, and Calcium. The Vitamin K in these vegetables help with clotting factors for blood; they also help detox the liver.

Dark colored fruits/veggies (Blue/purple) have antioxidant properties which are high in Vitamin C. It improves skin health and prevents wrinkles. Blue/Purple vegetables aid in the circulation of the veins to help prevent varicose veins.

White/Colorless vegetables aid in helping bone formation and growth and reducing osteoporosis, helps with cholesterol, helps support the immune system, supports eye health.

Directions:

Massage Kale with olive oil and salt, to soften. Add rest of ingredients to salad and enjoy.

Tuna & Avocado Salad

Ingredients:

> 1 can Light Tuna
> 1 Avocado
> 2 TBs Plain Vegenaise/Mayonnaise
> 1 tsp Lemon Juice
> Optional: Yellow pepper

Directions:

Open and Drain tuna and put in medium sized mixing bowl. Cut avocado in half length wise. Add the vegenaise/mayonnaise and lemon juice and pepper if desired and stir.

In Addition:

*Studies and FDA show that women, who are pregnant and eat certain types of tuna, are at a higher risk for Methyl-Mercury poisoning. Methylmercury is a neurotoxin that can be harmful to the brain and nervous system if a person is exposed to too much of it. Remember, that contaminated fish has an adverse effect on fertility. However, it is very important if you choose to eat canned tuna to choose Light and not to eat any more than twice a week.

Southwest Lime Taco Salad

Ingredients:

- 1 Portabella Mushroom
- 1 ear Fresh Corn or ½ package of ORGANIC Frozen Corn(cooked)
- 1 Avocado
- 1 Roma Tomato
- 2 TBS Mild Salsa
- 1 bag White Bean Chips
- 1 tsp Sea Salt
- 1 tsp Pepper
- 1-2 Garlic Cloves
- Other desired seasonings
- ¼ cup Almond Milk

Directions:

On a plate slice mushrooms into bite size pieces. Add corn. Cut ½ the avocado lengthwise. Cut the avocado and peel and add to the plate. Bring the salsa to spice it up.

In a blender, add other ½ of avocado, almond milk, garlic, pepper and salt. Add your Lime dressing to the mix and Enjoy. Party On!!

Thanks to Tasha Edwards for the original idea

Why these ingredients?

- Avocado is a source of good fats.
- Mushrooms are hearty and make you feel full quicker. Careful, because mushrooms belong to the fungi family and could cause other problems, such as yeast if consumed in excess.
- Garlic is an antifungal, antiviral that helps to boost the immune system and fight disease.

Prep Time: 30 mins
Cook Time: 15 mins

Curry Chicken Salad

Ingredients:

1 package Free Range Chicken (Legs), or whole Rotisserie Chicken cooked
Desired Seasonings
1 tsp Coconut Oil
1 tsp Vegenaise/Mayonnaise
Sliced Almonds
1 stalk celery
1 Tbs Yellow Curry

Optional:

Dried Cranberries, craisins, Relish

Directions:

Cut skin off and rinse 3-4 chicken legs. Add desired seasonings, and let marinate for approximately 30-45 minutes in refrigerator. Can either sauté or bake the chicken. Bake it on 325° for 30 minutes until it is done in the middle or if sautéing until the chicken is done or white in color. Cut meat off bones, if it's not already falling off and put in a large bowl. Chop celery and add in. Add in coconut oil, and relish. This recipe was so good, very flavorful, tender, and juicy. Make you wanna suck the bone, it's so good!!

You can serve atop a bed of spinach or mixed salad, croissant, with crackers, or it can accompany organic potato chips, or organic fruit, and soup. Very versatile.

Thanks to Spencer Thomas of Charlotte, NC

• Dried Cranberries are good for kidney health and are a source of fiber.

Yummy Lentil Salad

1 cup of any color Lentils or prepackaged ready to use Lentils

2 handfuls of Organic Spinach

1 Roma Tomato

½ Lemon

1 tsp of Honey or Agave

Directions:

Wash off spinach and be sure to pat dry. Slightly warm lentils to desired temperature; if using pre-packaged ready to use lentils. If not, boil lentils, until soft. Add Lentils to spinach. Squeeze lemon, being cautious of seeds into small glass mixed with honey or agave, then pour on top of salad or can add olive oil instead of honey/agave..Very good and nutritious!

There are other legumes that can be easily digested and absorbed as well such as Ad(z)uki beans and Mung Beans

Notes: Lentils are in the legume family. Often times, people can get gas from eating lentils or other vegetables. A way to prevent this is to soak the vegetable(s) in Kombu, which is a type of seaweed. This takes out the sulfur that is found in many vegetables that cause gas. In this case Soaking the Lentils overnight improves digestibility because the gas causing enzyme and trisaccharides are released in the soaked water or Kombu. Can cook the vegetable with the Kombu or discard. There are other legumes that can be easily digested and absorbed as well such as Ad(z)uki beans and Mung Beans

Sweet Antioxidant Salad

Ingredients:

3-5 Carrots (Orange, Purple, Yellow)

Few sprigs of Thyme

Juice of ½ Lemon

1tsp of Organic Apple Cider Vinegar

1 tsp Earth Balance Butter

1 tsp Local/Organic Honey

Desired Seasonings (Salt, Pepper)

Directions:

Wash off carrots. Thinly peel carrots lengthwise, using a vegetable peeler. Sprinkle seasonings, add butter, squeeze lemon, add apple cider vinegar, and add honey to carrots. De-stem thyme, and add to mixture. Let seasonings and liquids marinate in the carrots in refrigerator for at least 30 minutes or up to 24 hours.

In Addition:

- Thyme is a great antimicrobial and antibacterial herb. This herb can be used to help decrease coughs, treat respiratory infections, and help open sinuses. Thyme can also help decrease gas/bloating. Thyme is a very powerful herb. Be careful not to add too much.
- Carrots have what is called carotenoids. Carotenoids help with vison from Vitamin A to form the rods and cones that help us see color in our eyes. Carrots are an alkaline forming food, which help clear acne. Carrots can aid in urinary tract infections, skin lesions, and in the lungs because of the anti-inflammatory properties. Carrot juice when applied topically can help with burns. Carotenoids rely on fats in the diet to help get absorbed so be sure to add some oils to your meal. When combined with beets, carrots can help hormone regulation during menopause.

Healthy Crumble Crunch Salad

Ingredients:

1 package Ground Turkey
1 package Nitrate Free Turkey Bacon
1 tsp Extra Virgin Olive Oil
1 tsp Sunflower Kernels
1 tsp Sliced Almonds

1 package Organic Spinach

Directions:

Season Ground turkey, add ½ tsp olive oil. Place in refrigerator for approximately 30 minutes to let seasonings settle in. Cook 2 strips of Nitrate Free Bacon in pan. In a separate pan, cook the Ground Turkey with the remainder of olive oil. Once done, place atop a bed of spinach, crumble bacon, add kernels, and almonds. Drizzling with one of the following Salad Dressings from Page 33 will be an added touch: Olive Oil& Lemon Juice, Balsamic Vinegar, Red Wine Vinegar,

In **Addition**:

- Why Nitrate Free Turkey Bacon? Nitrate is another word for preservatives to prolong food freshness, while harmful chemicals are injected. Nitrates also contribute to Stomach Cancers.

Soups & Stews

Southern Turkey Gumbo

Ingredients:

¼ lb Deli Turkey(sliced thick)

½ Onion (cubed)

½ cup Brown Rice

2 Stalks Celery*

1lb Fresh Okra+ or frozen

1 fl. oz Chicken Broth or Vegetable Broth

1 Cup Water

2 Bouillon Cubes

2 Chicken Bouillon Cubes

1tsp Turmeric

Optional: Tomato

Directions:

Pour liquid ingredients into a crockpot. Add in Brown Rice. Cut the Turkey into cubes and add in. Remove the leaves from the Celery and slice horizontal. Put all ingredients in crockpot. Slice okra (be reminded that it will be extra slimy if rinsed too much) and add. Slice onion and add in. Cook on low for approximately 4-6 hours in Crockpot.

*Celery is an anti-inflammatory and is a source of good fiber (soluble), and helps to reduce blood pressures and Diabetes II.

+Okra is a source of Magnesium (one of the important minerals that our body needs). A deficiency in magnesium can cause spasms, conditions with the heart muscle, migraine headaches, and fatigue, to name a few conditions.

Prep Time: 20 minutes
Cook Time: 4-6 hours in Crockpot

Savory Lentil Soup

Ingredients:

Cook Time: 2-4 hrs in crockpot

- 1 package pre-cooked Lentils
- ½ fl. oz Vegetable Broth
- Approximately 5 carrots (chopped)
- Handful Dried Sage
- 1tsp Salt

Directions:

In a crockpot, add the above ingredients. Cook on low for approximately 2-4 hours.

Lentils are a source of Zinc, Iron, and Phosphorus just to name a few minerals in the body, but don't fret, you are probably not deficient of Phosphorus, because we consume much of it in our regular diets.

Sage is an herb for memory, and also helps for sore throats. Sage is very aromatic as well.

Fall Squash and Okra Soup

Ingredients:

    1 carton of Butternut Squash Soup

    1 handful okra

    ½ carton Vegetable Broth

    1 cup Brown Rice

    Pumpkin Cornbread Croutons

    Desired seasonings

Directions:

Do not rinse okra too much prior to slicing, it is slimy enough! Chop okra into small pieces. Turn pot on medium heat and add butternut squash. Add in okra, and desired seasonings. In another pot, pour vegetable broth and let come to a boil. Add in brown rice and let cook until tender. Once tender and the broth has cooked down, add rice to soup. Top with Croutons. MMMmm good on a cool day!

Cabbage Steamy Stew

Ingredients:

      1 head Fresh Cabbage

      1 handful Fresh Okra

      1 Handful Fresh Collard Greens

      1 mini Eggplant

      1 Tbsp Earth Balance Butter

      1 sauce cup of EVOO(Extra Virgin Olive Oil)

      1 Tbsp water

      Desired Seasonings (sea salt)

Directions:

Wash off and clean Collard Greens. Once washed off, start with the largest leaf and continue to stack leaves from largest to smallest. Roll the leaves together and slice. Add to pot of water and butter. Cut cabbage lengthwise and add to pot. Let these come to a boil, and add in seasonings. After approximately 10 minutes, chop up okra and add to mixture. While this is cooking, wash and dry off egg plant. Cut off ends. Slice lengthwise, and brush on EVOO and sprinkle with sea salt. Grill until discoloration happens. Add to mixture once done. It was very good!!

Fun Facts:

Cabbage is a really good vegetable and has many uses. Cabbage is high in Vitamin C, more than oranges. The outer leaves contain Vitamin E which helps to beautify the skin, and also contain more Calcium than the inner leaves. Cabbage is used for treating ulcers, constipation, the common cold, chronic cold feet, depression, and irritability.

Chicken Sausage Soup

Ingredients:

Prep Time: 20 mins
Cook Time: 20-30 mins

- 1 package Chicken Sausage
- 2 Yellow Organic Squash
- 2 Zucchini
- 1-2 Garlic Cloves
- ½ Onion
- 1 tsp EVOO (Extra Virgin Olive Oil) or Coconut Oil
- 1 tsp Butter
- ¼ cup Water

Optional: Use green cabbage in place of zucchini

Directions:

On medium heat, put butter, olive oil or coconut oil, and water in pot and let it come it a small boil. Slice Zucchini and Squash and add to pot. Cut up Chicken Sausage and add in pot. Cook for 20 minutes on medium heat. Once everything is finished cooking add the liquid from your pot into your bowl for a delectable soup!!

Thanks to Dwayne Deloatch of Greensboro, NC for the original recipe

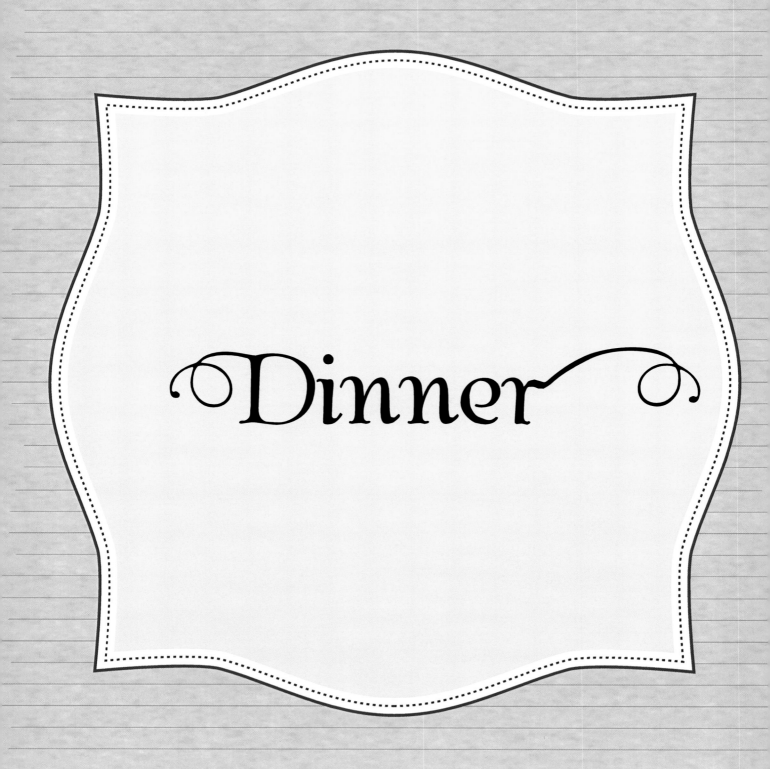

Dinner

Southwest Quesadilla

Ingredients:

2 Brown Rice Tortillas
1 Tbsp Guacamole
1 Tsp Mango Salsa
Deli Sliced Turkey
Soy Cheese

1Tsp Earth Balance Butter

Directions:

In medium sauce pan, add butter and let melt. Then add 1 tortilla. While the tortilla is browning, add turkey, guacamole, and cheese. Top the turkey and cheese and flip the tortilla to let the other side brown. While this is occurring, slightly open the top tortilla and add mango salsa. A good twist to the alternative.

Spaghetti Boat with Chicken

This is a healthy alternative to pasta. Oh, how we love our pasta. Pasta is one of my favorite meals (Lasagna specifically), however it is not always the healthiest choice, because it is a carbohydrate/starch that can turn into sugar once broken down in the body. To save time, use shrimp, for a healthier choice use the chicken.

Ingredients:

4 Boneless Chicken Breasts
1 Small Spaghetti Squash (yellow)
Garlic
Basil
Salt/pepper, turmeric, chicken flavored bouillon
Parmesan cheese
½ juice of Lemon
2 Tbsp. Butter
Olive Oil

½ Bunch Fresh Broccoli

Directions:

Wash outside of spaghetti squash. Poke a few holes in spaghetti squash using a knife and place in microwave for approximately 2 minutes to soften. Once softened, cut spaghetti squash lengthwise and scrap out the stringy contents and seeds. Drizzle 1 Tbsp Olive oil on inside of spaghetti squash and place in shaved side face down in oven on 350° for approximately 30-45 minutes. While cooking, cook chicken in skillet along with garlic and basil. When done, squash will be slightly dark on rim of squash, and yellow part of squash will be slightly darker. Let cool for 5 minutes. Scrape inside of spaghetti squash with a fork to get the spaghetti noodle look. The shaved hull can serve as a bowl to eat the spaghetti from.

Notes:

Spaghetti squash contains a wide range of vitamins which include A, most of the B vitamins, and Vitamin K. A report from Colorado State University explains that obtaining your daily vitamins through food sources such as spaghetti squash may be more beneficial than taking vitamin supplements. The most predominant mineral is Manganese which is needed to help bone production.

Prep Time: 10-15 minutes
Cook Time: 45 minutes

59

Not your Average Grilled Cheese

Ingredients:

1 package Croissant rolls
1 package slice Soy cheese (Daiya)
1 package Veggie Bacon
1Tbs Honey Butter
1tsp Earth Balance Butter (EBB)
*Some Morning Star brands have eggs in many of their products, so beware if you are Vegan.

Directions:

In a medium sized skillet, add 2-4 strips of bacon until desired texture is achieved. Add EBB. Cut croissant in half and add honey butter. Put top part face up in skillet. Add cheese. Once cheese has melted, break bacon into pieces and add to sandwich. Place the other side of the croissant atop and flip over, and let other side brown. So savory and good!!

61

Mushroom Infused Turkey Burger

Ingredients:

  1 Package Ground Turkey

  1 Portabella Mushroom

  1-2 Garlic Cloves

  1 Shallot/Onion

  1 Tbsp Mayonnaise/Vegenaise

  1 pkg. Hamburger Buns

  1 pkg. Fresh Broccoli

  2 Tbsp Mushroom Broth

  1 Tbsp Extra Virgin Olive Oil

  1 tsp Salt

  1 tsp Pepper

Optional Condiments:

  Cheese

  Nitrate Free Turkey Bacon

  Avocado

Directions:

Chop mushroom into quarter sizes. Peel garlic and shallot/onion. In a food processor, lightly pulse the mushroom, garlic, and shallot/onion. In a large bowl add the mixture. Add in Ground Turkey. Add mushroom broth, salt, and pepper. Mix with hands, folding in all ingredients. Divide into 4 equal parts and form a medium sized patty in hands. Place patties on a plate and chill in refrigerator for approximately 30 minutes. While patties chill, steam broccoli on medium heat. After approximately 10 minutes, add desired seasonings.

Once Turkey Patty is out of the refrigerator, cook on medium heat in frying pan with Olive Oil or place in oven on 350°. Flip once, cook until thoroughly done......So Good, and Moist!!

Prep Time: 20 minutes
Cook Time: 30-45 mins

Stuffed Turkey Meatballs with Cabbage and Rice

Ingredients:

½ Pkg. Green Peas

1lb Ground Turkey

1 1/2Tbsp Olive Oil

1 Egg

1 tsp Sea Salt

Suggested seasonings: Garlic Powder, Salt, Pepper,

1 head Green Cabbage

3 cups water

Brown Rice *

1 Tbsp Earth Balance Butter

Directions:

In a pot, boil peas for approximately 5 minutes. Drain and season with sea salt. Add in ½ tsp olive oil, seasonings and cooked peas. Form mixture into palm size balls. Add in remainder of olive oil in pan. In a separate pot, put in a small amount of olive oil, ½ cup water and chopped cabbage. Bring to a boil/simmer, adding in desired seasonings. In a separate pot, boil water, and add in brown rice. Once simmered, add in butter. …Pretty tasty, quick dinner.

*Brown rice is a source of zinc

Prep Time: 20 minutes
Cook Time: 20 minute

65

Side Dishes

Quinoa and Chopped Vegetables

Ingredients:

1 cup Quinoa

1 small head Red Cabbage

1 small head Green Cabbage

1 Red Onion

1 Red Pepper

1 Yellow Pepper

2 cups Water

1 Tbsp Butter

Desired Seasonings

Directions:

Boil quinoa in 1 1/2 cups water. *You know it is ready when there is foam around the pot, and the quinoa is fluffy (unlike rice). While the quinoa is cooking, chop up cabbage into small strips, and put in pot with the butter and remainder of the water. When majority of water is evaporated, add in seasonings. Cut up cabbage into pieces, and cut up red pepper

Did you know?? That Quinoa (pronunciation Keen-wah), is another Super Food and is a very good source of protein, high in fiber, and contains the essential amino acids that our body needs. Quinoa is a source of most of our B vitamins and minerals such as Magnesium, zinc, and has antioxidant properties, which reduce inflammation and help prevent disease. Quinoa keeps blood sugar levels balanced and reduces blood sugar levels to prevent Diabetes type II. Quinoa reduces migraine headaches because of Vitamin B2(Riboflavin) which promotes blood vessel expansion in the brain.

"Not ya momma's" Red Beans and Rice

Ingredients:

½ package of Red Lentils*

2 Tbsp Apple Cider Vinegar (ACV)

4 Handfuls Organic Spinach

1 cup Vegetable broth

1 cup Brown Rice

Desired Seasonings

Directions:

Soak lentils in ACV or Kombu for approximately 30 minutes. While this is soaking, bring Vegetable broth to a boil and add rice. While the rice is boiling, sauté the spinach in a small skillet. Make sure to season. While the rice is boiling and as the liquid starts to evaporate, add in desired seasonings.

*Can get red, and yellow lentils at International Markets

Delicious Broccoli and Carrot Slaw

Ingredients:

1 bunch Fresh Broccoli

1-2 Large Carrots

½ cup Onion

½ cup Craisins (optional)

1 tsp Mayonnaise/Veganaise

½ Lemon Juice

Optional: Nuts of your choice

Directions:

Wash vegetables in vegetable wash or Vinegar and water for about 2 minutes to get excess dirt and pesticides off. Rinse off with water. Cut the heads off of broccoli and place in a large mixing bowl. Cut carrots horizontally and add in bowl. Cut onion into small cubes and add in. Stir in mayonnaise/Vegenaise. Squeeze juice from lemon in. Mix thoroughly until everything is coated with mayonnaise/vegaenaise. Enjoy!

Crunchy Apple & Jicama Salad

Ingredients:

½ Jicama
Carrot (Yellow, Orange, Purple)
1 Tbs Honey
Sunflower seeds
Handful Spinach
½ cup Broccoli
½ cup Edamame
1 inch Ginger
½ juice of Lemon

1 Apple

Directions:

Wash off spinach, add to plate. Cut up jicama, carrot, ginger, and apple into desirable pieces, and add to spinach. Boil edamame lightly, drain water and salt lightly. Add to combination. Wash off broccoli, chop to make broccoli spears. Top combination with sunflower seeds, ½ juice of lemon, and honey. A perfect crunchy snack.

- Jicama has the taste of an apple, but less sweet.

- Sunflower Seeds contain most B vitamins, vitamin E, tryptophan, a good source of Omega-6 and aids in PMS symptoms. Minerals that are found in this seed are Zinc, copper

- Edamame is a source of protein.

Incredible Hulk

Ingredients:

½ Avocado
½ Cucumber
1 tsp Salt
1 tsp Pepper
1 head of Broccoli
½ package Edamame
juice of ½ Lime
1 Tbs olive oil

Directions:

Slice avocacado, cucumber, and broccoli and place on a plate. Boil edamame for approximately 5-10 minutes. Add to mixture. Squeeze lime and add olive oil.

Notes: Cucumbers reduce swellings, lifts depression, and purifies the skin.

Yam sandwich

Ingredients:

1 Yam

Slices of Mozzarella or Swiss cheese, or Dairy Alternative cheese

Handful of Spinach

1 Tbs Mayonnaise, or Balsamic Vinegar as a spread

Salt

1 tsp Cinnamon

Bread

1 TBs Cranberry confit

Optional:

Tomato, or Arugula.

Directions:

Wash off yam/sweet potatoe. Place on Parchment Paper and drizzle with Coconut Oil. Roast yam/sweet potatoe for approximately 30 minutes on 375°. Peel and unwrap yam/sweet potatoe. Mash yam, add salt. Once mashed, add desired condiment, spinach,Cheese, Confit, and Yam to a slice of bread. A unique sandwich!!

Cranberry Confit (jam)

1 package of fresh cranberries

1/2 cup Orange Juice or Lemon Juice

Vanilla bean(seeds)

Put all ingredients in a pot and start the boiling process on low with a lid, until this gelatinous jam reduces. Once this happens, remove lid so the water can evaporate.

Did you know? Yams help to beautify the skin, helps to increase the quality of milk for lactating mothers, and they aid in menopause.
Cranberries aid in urinary health

Prep Time: 15 minutes
Cook Time: 30 minutes

75

Snacks

Protein Packed Apple Cake

Ingredients:

2 Brown Rice Cakes
1 Tbsp Sunflower Butter
1 Organic Red Apple
Cinnamon

Directions:

Add any nut butter to rice cakes and enjoy this "hold over" snack. Chop up apple of choice into wedges and sprinkle cinnamon on top. A healthy, complete snack.

More Information:

Why not Peanut Butter? Peanut Butter has what is called Aflotoxins. Aflotoxins are a type of mold that the body does not digest well.

Veggie Trail Mix

Ingredients:

Dried Okra

Dried Green Beans

Dried Carrots

Dried Edamame

*Eat this in place of potato chips, it adds a good crunch to your day.

Homemade Trail Mix

Ingredients:

2 tsp Honey Sunflower Kernels

2 tsp Black Bean Sesame sticks

2 tsp slivered almonds

2 tsp salted cashews

Directions:

Mix together and put in glass Tupperware

*Almonds and Cashews are great sources of protein

Veggie Chips, Better than your Regular Chips!

Kale Chips

Ingredients:

1 bunch Kale

1 TBs Extra Virgin Olive Oil

1 tsp Sea Salt

Directions:

Wash kale thoroughly, then chop up. Place on baking sheet, and pour Olive Oil over Kale. prinkle with salt. Bake in oven at 350° for approximately 15-20 minutes. Good. Crispy Snack. Good replacement for Potato Chips

Oven Baked Squash Chips

Ingredients

1 Round Green Zuccini Squash

1 Egg

Panko Bread Crumbs

Desired Seasonings

Directions: Wash off squash. Slice into small circles. With the sliced squash, put both sides in egg bowl. Then put both sides in Bread Crumbs. Add to a cookie sheet. Bake on 350° for approximately 20 minutes. Around 10 minutes, flip over and let cook on other side. Once slightly brown, take out and sprinkle with desired seasonings.

Tantalizing Yogurt Toppings

Here are some ideas to add to plain yogurt:

Dark Organic Honey
Granola
Some type of nut
Cinnamon
Fresh Fruit

Additional Information:

- Cinnamon is good for the heart

- Yogurt has Vitamin K, which is good for intestinal bacteria that our gut needs to keep us healthy and help fight off bad bugs that tend to get in our gut.

- Nuts are a type of protein that will sustain you for at least a couple of hrs.

References:

Hudson, T. Dr. Women's Encyclopedia of Natural Medicine. 2nd Ed. McGraw Hill. New York. 2008.

Mahan. L and Raymond. J Krause's Food & The Nutrition Care process. 14th Ed. Elsevier. St. Louis, MO.2017

Marz and Russell. Medical Nutrition.: 2nd Ed. Omni Press. Portland, OR. 1999

Pitchford. P Healing with Whole Foods; Asian Traditions and Modern Nutrition. 3rdEd. North Atlantic Books. Berkeley, CA. 2002

Zhang. Ping A comprehensive handbook for Traditional Chinese Medicine & Facial Acupuncture.1st Ed. Nefeli Corp Publications. Port Washington, NY. 2006

www.fda.com/nutriton.

www.sciencedirect.com/science/article

www.ncbi.nlm.nih.gov/pubmed. Connelly NA, and Bruce Lauber T, and Niederdeppe J, Knuth BA. (Fish Consumption among Women anglers of Childbearing Age). 2016.

www.coconutresearchcenter.org. Fife, Bruce. ND. (Coconut The Tree of Life). 2015

NOTES:

About the Author

During Chérie's abroad studies in Copenhagen Denmark, she became interested in cooking and learning about foods from other cultures. She has taken the accumulation of her life experiences from growing up in North Carolina, to her professional training in Pharmacy, Medical and Nutritional training, as she now finishes her training to become an Acupuncturist (2017). As a student she created many of these meals knowing that fast food was not the healthy way to go.

Her medical training has allowed her to delve deeper into various ways of helping people become healthy through this publicaton of Healthy Never Tasted So Good. In her book she demonstrates the health benefits of eating fresh and organic foods with quick and easy meals.

Contact Info: 910.707.4602
cheriemonet2231@gmail.com

Edwards Brothers Malloy
Ann Arbor MI. USA
April 10, 2017